FRANCISCAN
WISDOM

THE ESSENTIAL TEACHINGS
OF SAINT FRANCIS OF ASSISI

FRANCISCAN
WISDOM

INTRODUCTION AND BIOGRAPHY
BY MATTHEW KELLY

BLUE SPARROW
North Palm Beach, Florida

BLUE
sparrow

Copyright © 2021
Kakadu, LLC
Published by BLUE SPARROW

The quotes in this book have been drawn from dozens
of sources. They are assumed to be accurate as quoted in
their previously published forms. Although every effort
has been made to verify the quotes and sources, the
Publisher cannot guarantee their perfect accuracy.

Design by Kara Ebert
ISBN: 978-1-63582-168-0 (hardcover)
ISBN: 978-1-63582-169-7 (e-Book)

10   9   8   7   6   5   4   3   2   1

Printed in the United States of America

FIRST EDITION

INTRODUCTION

THERE IS ONE IDEA that wins me daily to Christianity: It works. There are two millennia of proof. Christianity has been bringing the best out of people on every continent and in every place and time since Jesus walked the earth. It has never been tried and found wanting. Whenever the Gospel has been authentically adopted and lived it has been an awe-inspiring and positive influence in the world.

It is not without its critics of course. But critics of Christianity always cite Christians who failed or refused to allow the Gospel to transform their hearts and direct their actions. These personal failures of individuals are not a failure of the Gospel. The Gospel works.

Whenever and wherever men and women have tried to live out the central premises of the Gospel, the betterment of the individual and humanity has always followed. This quest to embrace the fullness of the Gospel in our own place, time, and way, is the quest for holiness. When we place this quest at the center of our daily activity, our lives and relationships thrive.

This world can be dark and ugly, but holiness is beauty and light. There is nothing more attractive than holiness. This has been one of the touchstone ideas of my spiritual journey. It encourages me, it challenges me, it reminds me.

Each day we have questions and face problems. Holiness is the answer to every question and the solution to every problem. But we have wandered far from this wisdom. Grappling with a question, we don't ask: How would holiness answer this question? Faced with a problem, we don't ask: How would holiness solve this problem?

We refuse to acknowledge, accept, and embrace the universal answer to our questions and solution to our problems. Holiness is the rejected solution. The dissatisfaction of our lives proves this and measures the extent to which we have rejected this truth.

There are no new questions, and we are bored with the old answers. Whether or not these ancient answers are true doesn't figure into our modern reasoning.

Still, in every place and every time, there are a few brave souls who hold to the Gospel like their lives depend upon it, and they shine for all to see.

There's nothing more attractive than holiness. This single idea wins me to faith anew each day. Francis of Assisi stands as a singular example of this piercing truth. This man and his life are universally intriguing and attractive. For eight hundred years, he has been loved and respected by men and women of all faiths, and those of no faith. His holiness crosses the bounds of religion and prejudice.

At the same time, Francis is one among many, each an arresting example of the potency and timelessness of the Gospel.

Most holy people live in plain sight. We cross paths with them every day. They will never be recognized officially as saints, and they prefer that. I have known many holy people. Most of them lived quiet, diligent lives, dedicated to serving other people. They became extraordinary people by repeatedly doing the ordinary things with great love.

Our lives become animated by faith when we discover once and for all that we too can walk that path. Holiness is possible. Not just for people in far off places and times, but you and me, here and now. And not only is holiness possible, but it is needed.

The extraordinary men and women we are exploring in this series have been raised up by God in their own places and times to serve humanity in specific and powerful ways. Their legacies and examples echo on throughout the ages. Our curiosity should lead us to ask: Although they were very different people with very different missions, what is the defining characteristic that binds them together? Availability is the answer. They made themselves one hundred percent available to God.

Francis of Assisi, Ignatius, Dominic, Benedict, and Teresa of Avila made themselves completely available to God. It was complete surrender to the will of God that allowed him to work so powerfully through them.

The result was a contagious passion for life. They were fully alive and fully human, and that was phenomenally attractive to people.

Their lives stand today as an invitation. It is an invitation to wholeness. It is a radical invitation to everything you yearn for that you don't know you need and want. An invitation to find your best, truest, highest, and most authentic self in Jesus.

They each had to stop resisting what they really needed. They each had to stop wrestling for what they didn't really want. Only then were they able to see that God wanted to give them everything they needed. Only then were they able to see that what they really wanted was what God wanted for them all along.

Now it is your turn.

We want an easier way, but there is no easy way. And the most difficult path to walk in this life is any path other than the one God calls you to.

The Gospel is not vague. It leads us along a narrow

path. The lives of the saints also point out the narrow path with startling clarity. Their times, like ours, were starving for authenticity. Their times, like ours, were hungry for truth. Our time, like theirs, needs brave men and women to answer the call.

What does the world need? Truth, beauty, goodness, and light. Fill your life with these and spread them wherever you go.

MATTHEW KELLY

BIOGRAPHY

OF

SAINT FRANCIS OF ASSISI

AT THE DAWN of the thirteenth century, the world was experiencing two problems that were very similar to those it faces today. First, coins were being mass-produced, and as a result were quickly becoming the primary medium of exchange. This general introduction of money was creating a greed and materialism that had not existed except among the elite under the bartering system. People had never hoarded eggs or grain or chickens, because they could not be stored for long periods of time without rotting or dying. But coins were cold and lifeless, and could be easily stored. Thus, the desire to amass wealth began to seduce the human heart more than ever before. The second problem of the day was that religion had become more of a habit and an empty tradition than a genuine conviction. Sound familiar?

In 1182, a child was born in the tiny town of Assisi, in the hills of Northern Italy. With his life, this child would address both the greed and the religious decay that plagued his day. His extraordinary example has never stopped inspiring us.

The boy's name was Francesco (or Francis); he was the son of a wealthy cloth merchant. While his parents hoped he would go on to great things, perhaps become a mayor or an influential businessman, Francis seemed to waste the first twenty years of his life indulging in parties and daydreams of becoming a great knight.

Francis was a leader and a favorite among the young people of his hometown. The life of every party, he spent endless nights in the frivolous pursuit of wine, song, and dance. Full of charm and wit, he was loved by all.

At twenty years of age, Francis decided he was ready to embrace what he believed to be his chance at greatness. He left Assisi in full armor, upon the finest horse, to take part in the battle between Assisi and nearby Perugia.

During the battle, Francis was knocked from his horse and later captured by the enemy. As the son of a wealthy man, he was held hostage for ransom. Only after several months was he released, and by this time he had become very ill.

His convalescence provided the necessary meeting ground for him to encounter God. Within this stillness and solitude his heart began to soften and transform. Though he recovered from his grave illness, Francis would never again be the frivolous fun-seeker the people of Assisi had come to know and love. All his glory seeking had revealed to him a profound dissatisfaction, a restlessness lurking in his soul that would not be ignored. While in his former life he wasted countless hours with crowds of rowdy friends, now he sought the solitude of time alone in the quiet fields that surrounded Assisi.

A turning point in his new life occurred one day when he visited the abandoned and dilapidated church of San Damiano, not far from Assisi.

Entering the weary structure, he knelt before the crucifix to pray. At that moment, Francis heard a voice speak to him, saying, "Rebuild my Church. As you can see, it is in ruins."

Believing he had heard the voice of God, Francis set about rebuilding the crumbling church of San Damiano. Using materials bought with his father's money or begged from the people of Assisi, Francis fully restored the little church with his own hands. He then set about rebuilding the abandoned church of Saint Peter, and finally restored the also dilapidated Portiuncula, which later became the center of life for Francis and his brothers.

Once the Portiuncula was completed, Francis again heard the voice of God, saying, "Francis, rebuild my Church. As you can see, it is in ruins." On this occasion, his heart was opened to understand that God was not calling him to a life of physical labor rebuilding churches. But rather, he was calling Francis to a spiritual mission.

Francis then turned his back on all worldly wealth to embrace a life of simplicity, humility, poverty, and prayer.

His spirit of uncompromising commitment to the Gospel has remained a force of renewal in the Church in every place and time for more than seven hundred years. Francis of Assisi has endured as one of the most intriguing figures in human history. Today there are more than one million Franciscan friars and brothers around the world. Have you ever tried to get people to volunteer for a couple of hours? Imagine inspiring more than a million people to give their whole lives for a cause.

During his lifetime, this little man of poverty became and continues to be a worldwide influence. He has inspired and influenced the great thinkers of every age. He is the subject of hundreds of books, thousands of studies, numerous motion pictures and documentaries, and a myriad of musical compositions honoring his life. If you travel the world, you will come upon countless rivers, mountains, roads, and even cities named after Francis, the most famous of which is, of course, San Francisco.

He has been hailed by historians, praised by religious leaders of all beliefs, and quoted by presidents. He has inspired artistic masterpieces including works by Rembrandt, who was by his own admission an anti-Catholic Protestant, yet he was enamored of the life and virtue of Francis. It was Francis who invented the crèche, or Nativity scene, to draw attention to the powerful paradox of God's son being born into the poverty of a stable. Every year, millions of families unconsciously honor the memory of Francis with the Nativity scenes they place in their homes. Recognized universally as a lover of nature, Francis is the statue most commonly placed in the garden.

He was all this in the past, and I believe he remains a powerful and trustworthy spiritual guide to the people of our own troubled times.

But what I delight in most about Francis is that the people who loved him honored him by remembering his story—all of his story, even his wild youth and his moments of impatience during the early days of his ministry. It is for this reason that biographers have been so successful at portraying Francis as a "whole man" rather than as a caricature of holiness. He was certainly saintly, but not sanctimonious. He loved God, but he also loved his neighbor and creation.

Francis was real. He was striving with all his heart to live an authentic life. And like the first Christians, he captured the imaginations and intrigued the hearts and minds of the people of his time and the people of times to come. Francis is a practical example of the power of one authentic life indelibly engraved upon history.

365 MOMENTS OF ESSENTIAL

FRANCISCAN WISDOM

1

—

I have been all things unholy.
If God can work through me,
He can work through anyone.

Saint Francis of Assisi

2

—

Who loves Francis of Assisi? Only
Christians? No. Men and women
of all faiths love Francis of Assisi.
There's something about his life that
is dripping with authenticity, and it
just attracts people. It gets them to
set their biases aside, to set their
prejudices aside, and realize, 'Wow,
this person was a great light in what is
sometimes a very dark world.'

Matthew Kelly

3

—

Lord, make me an instrument of your
peace.
Where there is hatred, let me sow love;
where there is injury, pardon;
where there is doubt, faith;
where there is despair, hope;
where there is darkness, light;
where there is sadness, joy.

Saint Francis of Assisi

4

—

I think the difference between
me and some people is that
I'm content to do my little bit.
Sometimes people think they
have to do big things in order
to make change. But if each one
would light a candle, we'd have a
tremendous light.

Thea Bowman

5

—

Do few things but do them well.
Simple joys are holy.

Saint Francis of Assisi

6

—

We are meant to be inspired, creative, supportive, optimistic people. If our lives don't feel this sweetness, we need liberation.

Jon M. Sweeney

7

—

The question Francis raises for us
and the lesson he comes to teach us
is that God is speaking to us through
our dissatisfaction. What is it that
you are dissatisfied with at this time
in your life? And what is God saying
to you through that dissatisfaction?

Matthew Kelly

8

—

The best portion of a good man's life:
his little, nameless, unremembered
acts of kindness and love.

William Wordsworth

9

—

Start by doing what's necessary, then do what's possible, and suddenly you are doing the impossible.

Saint Francis of Assisi

10

What the Franciscan charism is all about is relationship...What is my relationship to my sisters? The people I work with? To the people that I serve? To the world? Who am I in this world and what am I called to do? It's nothing big. It's relating on a one-to-one basis and doing what I can.

Ellen McCabe

11

—

Could a greater miracle take place than for us to look through each other's eyes for an instant?

Henry David Thoreau

12

Being heard is so close to being loved that for the average person, they are almost indistinguishable.

David Augsburger

13

—

If you have men who will exclude any of God's creatures from the shelter of compassion and pity, you will have men who will deal likewise with their fellow men.

Saint Francis of Assisi

14

—

Most men wanted war in those days... Francis wanted peace. Most men liked to see women kept in their places. Francis helped women define places of their own. Most people used plants and animals. Francis loved and cherished them.

Adrian House

15

All the darkness in the world
cannot extinguish the light
of a single candle.

Saint Francis of Assisi

16

—

Let us hear the same call
Francis heard: Go and rebuild
my church. Let us ask for his
prayers and let us follow his
example. We need saints
and heroes for this new
missionary age.

Keith Fournier

17

—

The most deadly poison of our times
is indifference.

Saint Maximilian Kolbe

18

———

In a materialistic world, where the meaning and measure of life is counted by the things we buy and the experiences we enjoy, the barefoot, raggedly robed Francis calls us to simplicity.

Mark Galli

19

___

What do you think about the most?
That's your treasure.

Justin Fatica

20

___

We all have a past—saints included—and very often we are not proud of every aspect of our past. Certainly Francis of Assisi would later weep for his unfaithfulness to God, but he did not remain paralyzed by his guilt. He moved forward and allowed God to love him despite his sinful past.

Joseph Mary Elder

21

What do you have to fear? Nothing.
Whom do you have to fear? No one.
Why? Because whoever has joined
forces with God obtains three great
privileges: omnipotence without
power, intoxication without wine,
and life without death.

Saint Francis of Assisi

22

Like St. Francis, God will very often call us out of our comfort zones in life. It is in such situations, where we feel inept, incompetent, and afraid, that we must rely on God to do what we cannot.

Joseph Mary Elder

23

——

Lord, help my to live this day,
quietly, easily. To lean upon
Thy great strength, trustfully,
restfully. To wait for unfolding of
Thy will, patiently, serenely. To
meet others, peacefully, joyously.
To face tomorrow, confidently,
courageously.

Saint Francis of Assisi

24

___

One scene depicts a nearly
naked Francis—the rich kid
tossing is fancy clothes to
his father—befuddling high
society by trading a life of
power and luxury for one of
simplicity and poverty.

Rick Steves

25

—

The question of what you want
to own is actually the question
of how you want to live your life.

Marie Kondō

26

———

Eight hundred years ago, this humble man transformed his world and renewed the Catholic Church by simple but revolutionary acts of practicing his faith as it had never been practiced before. Francis was a man of peace who was known for building bridges of communication, understanding, and cooperation between warring people, groups, and nations.

Victor Narro

27

In a gentle way,
you can shake the world.

Mahatma Ghandi

28

———

The role of the material and natural world is to arouse the human consciousness to praise God, and in turn, humanity is to serve nature by giving it a voice which would not otherwise be heard in the universe.

Bonaventure

29

——

The grand show is eternal.
It is always sunrise somewhere.

John Muir

30

With St. Francis of Assisi, gospel
simplicity reappeared upon the earth.

Paul Sabatier

31

Preach the Gospel at all times
and when necessary use words.

Saint Francis of Assisi

32

In the context of joy, I would like to…invite you to slow down, even if for a brief moment each day, and take in the nature that exists around you. When was the last time you experienced a sunset or sunrise without a smartphone or tablet in your hand?

Jason Lody

33

———

In our hectic lives, our unquenchable thirst for progress, possessions, money, and status, we forget the power of 'attention' to the ever present now. But without attention, we live only on the surface of existence. Attention allows us to listen, to see, to touch the heart of another and to be touched...So live like Francis—give your attention to listening inwardly, without judgment or resistance, to the present moment.

Marcella Nachreiner

34

—

Sooner or later we realize that what the world has to offer is simply not enough to satisfy us. It is only then that most of us turn to four of life's biggest questions: Who am I? What am I here for? What matters most? What matters least?

Matthew Kelly

35

Each of us enters the world of
possibility and of risk, of joy and
of sorrow, of happiness and of
pain. We enter this world without a
clear roadmap or instant access to
who we truly are and what we are
meant to do. It is a struggle indeed,
but...the struggle is at least not an
insurmountable struggle when we
recall as Saints Francis and Clare
did, that life is neither not all about
us nor...are we left alone to figure it
out.

Daniel Horan

36

———

Look at the birds of the air;
they do not sow or reap or store
away in barns, and yet your heavenly
Father feeds them. Are you not
much more valuable than they?

Matthew 6:26

37

___

As he said these words, all the
birds began to open their beaks, to
stretch their necks, to spread their
wings and reverently to bow their
heads to the ground, endeavouring
by their motions and by their
songs to manifest their joy to St.
Francis. And the saint rejoiced
with them. He wondered to see
such a multitude of birds, and
was charmed with their beautiful
variety...for all which he devoutly
gave thanks to the Creator.

Ugolino Brunforte

38

___

It's become so fashionable to talk about finding God in the ordinary that we run the risk of forgetting that, as Christians, our lives aren't supposed to be so ordinary that they're indistinguishable for everyone else's.

Susan Pitchford

39

————

The Lord has called me to
be a new kind of fool in this
world.

Saint Francis of Assisi

40

We anxiously grasp at the world, hoping that more stuff, more wealth, more power, and more acclaim will satisfy us. Despite the futility of the world, something tells us it will bring us ultimate rest, but it never does. The more we seek, the more we realize how unsatisfied we are... As disciples of Jesus, we must give up our restless anxiety and trust in God.

Casey Cole

41

—

As followers of most holy poverty, since they had nothing, they loved nothing; so they feared losing nothing.

Thomas of Celano

42

Not to hurt our humble brethren is our first duty to them, but to stop there is not enough. We have a higher mission—to be of service to them whenever they require it.

Saint Francis of Assisi

43

———

Francis was a great saint and a joyful
man. His simplicity, his humility,
his faith, his love for Christ, his
goodness towards every man and
every woman, brought him gladness
in every circumstance. Indeed,
there subsists an intimate and
indissoluble relationship between
holiness and joy.

Pope Benedict XVI

44

Somebody should tell us, right at the beginning of our lives, that we are dying. Then we might live life to the limit, every minute of every day. Do it! I say. Whatever you want to do, do it now! There are only so many tomorrows.

Pope Paul VI

45

———

All in all, listeners felt as if
something radically anew
was afoot—the beginning of a
religious awakening. Though all
of society believed in God, when
Francis spoke, it was as if God was
real for the first time.

Mark Galli

46

———

Francis faced some of the biggest
questions of his day: How to
respond to the growing gap
between rich and poor? How to
make peace between enemies?
What is our relationship to the
world God made? Where is God
when we suffer? Because these are
also the questions of our own day,
Francis has much to say to us.

John Hebenton

47

If God created shadows it was to
better emphasize the light.

Pope John XXIII

48

For Francis, Lady Poverty, as
he called her, was a precious
bride. Not because poverty
or destitution or homeless or
hunger is a value in itself but
because voluntary poverty—
poverty embraced—actually
can help us to recognize the
giftedness of all things.

Brother Samuel

49

—

Giving thanks warms the soul and reminds us that life is an extraordinary privilege. Joy doesn't come from having, but from appreciating what we have. You can possess all the treasures, pleasures, and blessings this world has to offer, but if you don't appreciate them they will never bring you any real satisfaction. Joy is the fruit of appreciation.

Matthew Kelly

50

___

People don't know how to live the moment. We're living yesterday. 'Why did I say that?' 'If only I didn't.' 'Maybe I should have.' But we can't change yesterday. We don't have a lot of power with tomorrow either. We can hope for it, but there's not one of us who are truly assured of it. All we have is now. And when we slow ourselves down to the now, we grab that energy.

Susan Pitchford

51

—

Can any one of you by worrying
add a single hour to your life?

Matthew 6:27

52

___

'Fraternity' is a St. Francis kind of
word. Treating earth's creatures as
brothers and sisters was a joyous
expression of the life he lived in
communion with the divine. And he
extended this fraternal care to not
just creatures. To Francis, the sun
was 'Brother Sun,' the moon 'Sister
Moon.' Likewise wind, water, and fire
were his siblings. Elemental forces
and living presences were to be
acknowledged as you would a friend.

Kennedy Warne

53

—

Those who look for the laws of nature
as a support for their new works
collaborate with the creator.

Antonio Gaudi

54

The image of Christ crucified
spoke to him. 'Francis,' it said,
calling him by name: 'go rebuild
My house; as you see, it is all being
destroyed.' Francis was more than
a little stunned, trembling, and
stuttering like a man out of his
senses. He prepared himself to
obey and pulled himself together
to carry out the command. He felt
this mysterious change in himself,
but could not describe it...

Thomas of Celano

55

___

The people of Assisi, including Francis's churchgoing parents, were aghast. Why had this merchant's son traded his fashionable clothes for the rags of a beggar? Why was this playboy hanging out with lepers? Had he lost his mind? The infectious, passionate, no-holds-barred faith of Francis soon ignited a movement of men and women who fanned out throughout Europe and the rest of the world.

John Michael Talbot

56

———

Someone once had a terribly beautiful thing to say about Jesus. This person wasn't even Christian. He said, 'The lovely thing about Jesus was that he was so at home with sinners, because he understood that he wasn't one bit better than they were.' We differ from others—from criminals, for example—only in what we do or don't do, not in what we are.

Anthony de Mello

57

___

The deeds you do may be the only
sermon some persons will hear
today.

Saint Francis of Assisi

58

St. Augustine of Hippo, writing,
long time before Francis, said
that God longs to give us
something. God longs to give
us the precious gift of himself,
but we're not able to receive it
because our hands
are already too full.

Brother Samuel

59

———

If we are not free to say no,
we are not free to say yes.

Matthew Kelly

60

———

Prayer enabled Francis of Assisi to see the connections in what otherwise could have been a very fragmented life: preacher, healer, leader of friars, spiritual guide for many lay people, and advisor to popes and bishops. Rather than ask how he could find time and energy to pray, Francis asked himself, 'How could I not pray?'

Pat McCloskey

61

—

Our labor here is brief, but the reward is eternal. Do not be disturbed by the clamor of the world, which passes like a shadow.

Saint Clare of Assisi

62

___

Prayer is ultimately about making
ourselves available to God.
So is life.

Matthew Kelly

63

___

Francis made his whole body a tongue; more than someone who prayed, he had become prayer.

Thomas of Celano

64

___

Praised be You, my Lord, with all your
creatures, especially Sir Brother Sun, Who
is the day and through whom You give us
light...Praised be You, my Lord, through
Sister Moon and the stars, in heaven
You formed them clear and precious
and beautiful. Praised be You, my Lord,
through Brother Wind, and through
the air, cloudy and serene, and every
kind of weather through which You give
sustenance to Your creatures. Praised be
You, my Lord, through Sister Water, which is
very useful and humble and precious and

Saint Francis of Assisi

65

_____

When you kneel before an altar,
do it in a way that others may be
able to recognize that you know
whom before you kneel.

Maximilian Kolbe

66

———

When he heard that the Gospel said not to possess money, wear shoes, or own more than one tunic, Francis obeyed. In addition, and just as important, he obeyed joyfully. There was a tremendous optimism and enthusiasm about Francis.

Conrad Harkins

67

———

For joy cannot be dissociated
from sharing. In God Himself,
all is joy because all is giving.

Pope Paul VI

68

———

I am as I am in the eyes of God.
Nothing more, nothing less.

Saint Francis of Assisi

69

In fact the more critical Francis became of himself, the more compassionate he was with others. The more impatient he was with himself, the more patient he was with others. The more darkness he found in himself, the more light he easily saw in those around him.

Bruce Davis

70

He did not try to build a new church, but he repaired an old one, restored an ancient one. He did not tear out the foundation, but he built upon it.

Thomas of Celano

71

———

You wouldn't abandon ship
in a storm just because you
couldn't control the winds.

Thomas More

72

———

What is it that stands higher than words? Action.

What is it that stands higher than action? Silence.

Saint Francis of Assisi

73

Prayer is the raising of the mind to God.
We must always remember this.
The actual words matter less.

Pope John XXIII

74

A former prisoner of war, someone who engaged in class fights as a youth, Francis knew what power could do to people. He knew what violence did to society. And he wanted to stand against it.

Casey Cole

75

No one is to be called an enemy.

Saint Francis of Assisi

76

———

I can hardly think of a spirituality
with a more positive outlook on
creation than the Franciscans.
More than just nature enthusiasts
or tree huggers, there is an acute
sense in our theology that the
immaterial, eternal God can
and has become present in the
material, finite world.

Casey Cole

77

——

Ask the beasts and they will teach
you the beauty of this earth.

Saint Francis of Assisi

78

——

Jesus is happy to come with us,
as truth is happy to be spoken,
as life is to be lived, as light to
be lit, as love is to be loved,
as joy to be given, as peace to
spread.

Saint Francis of Assisi

79

Faith is not a light which scatters
all our darkness, but a lamp
which guides our steps in
the night and suffices for the
journey.

Pope Francis

80

___

Usually when he saw a leper he would turn and go the other direction. This time he got off his horse and he went and he embraced the leper. And as Franciscans we look at that as really the pinnacle of his conversion—when he was able to recognize Jesus in the leper.

Ellen McCabe

81

—

Gestures, in love, are incomparably more attractive, effective and valuable than words.

François Rabelais

82

O Lord, do not let us turn into 'broken cisterns' that can hold no water...do not let us be so blinded by the enjoyment of the good things of earth that our hearts become insensible to the cry of the poor, of the sick, of orphaned children and of those innumerable brothers and sisters of ours who lack the necessary minimum to eat, to clothe their nakedness, and to gather their family together in one roof.

Pope John XXIII

83

———

It would be considered a theft on our part if we didn't give to someone in greater need than we are.

Saint Francis of Assisi

84

———

That blindness which constrains men to consecrate their hearts to material preoccupations, makes them slave to a few pieces of gold or a few acres of land, renders them insensible to the beauties of nature and deprives them of infinite joys.

Paul Sabatier

85

—

Do you have a healthy relationship with money? There are a thousand ways to have an unhealthy relationship with money. You can hoard it or waste it, use it to control others, or lust after more of it. The list goes on and on. There is one way to have a healthy relationship with money: Remember it is not yours. Everything belongs to God. The money and things we have he has simply entrusted to us.

Matthew Kelly

86

———

How many times every day is
Jesus waiting for us to recognize,
or to minister to Him, or to love
Him, and we don't because of our
fears, our prejudices, and our lack
of love?

Kevin J. Haines

87

———

To be Franciscan…is to be in
relationship with, rather than
to stand apart from, those who
are experiencing oppression,
marginalization, and all forms of
injustice.

Anonymous

88

Unlike most of his contemporaries, Francis taught that God calls humans to live with plants and animals, sun, wind, and rain not as masters or adversaries, but as brothers and sisters. As with siblings, it is a relationship of give and take.

Kathleen Manning

89

—

Let him who is the greatest
and has the right to command
consider himself as the lowest
and the servant of the other
brothers.

Saint Francis of Assisi

90

It is my hope that the inspiration of Saint Francis will help us to keep ever alive a sense of 'fraternity' with all those good and beautiful things which Almighty God has created. And may he remind us of our serious obligation to respect and watch over them with care.

Pope John Paul II

91

The only imperative that nature
utters is, 'Look. Listen. Attend.'

C. S. Lewis

92

He often called himself a juggler.
And what he loved to do was
to toss up in the air society's
most cherished possessions:
rank, wealth, power, sexuality,
reputation. And once they
were in the air, you could see
the undersides of them, and
very often the undersides—the
opposites—looked far more
attractive than those cherished
possessions.

Adrian House

93

___

Humility is the recognition of the truth about God and ourselves.

Saint Francis of Assisi

94

——

When you ponder and reflect
on the meaning of life, you're
really thinking about God, even
if you don't yet have a name
for Him. He's certainly thinking
about you.

Regis Martin

95

———

Heaven wheels above you, displaying
to you her eternal glories, and still
your eyes are on the ground.

Dante

96

Lord, give me a sense of humor
so that I may take some happiness
from this life and share it with others.

Thomas More

97

———

We are here to be witnesses of love and to celebrate life, because life has been created in the image of God. Life is to love and to be loved.

Mother Teresa

98

———

When we have fewer things,
we don't have to worry about
keeping them and maintaining
them. We have more space in our
lives to pay attention to a deeper
reality, the intrinsic value of God's
creation, and the needs of our
neighbors.

Dawn Nothwehr

99

———

He told them: 'Take nothing for your journey, neither a staff, nor a bag, nor bread, nor money; and do not even have two tunics apiece.'

Luke 9:3

100

———

Francis was dissatisfied. God used his dissatisfaction to invite him to go wild in a wonderful way by rebelling against the norms and expectations society had placed on him and his life.

Matthew Kelly

101

Poverty is the Franciscan symbol
of liberty, of freedom.

M. Michaeline

102

———

Francis and Clare's agenda for justice was the most foundational and undercutting of all others: a very simple lifestyle outside the system of production and consumption, plus a conscious identification with the marginalized of society. In this position you do not 'do' acts of peace and justice as much as your life itself is peace and justice.

Richard Rohr

103

Although I am not very familiar with
many Catholic saints, I do know
about St Francis, having visited
Assisi and attended inter-religious
gatherings there. His discipline, the
simplicity of his way of life and his
love for all creatures are qualities
that I find deeply inspiring.

The Dalai Lama

104

———

Above all the grace and the gifts
that Christ gives to his beloved
is that of overcoming self.

Saint Francis of Assisi

105

———

Worry is a weakness from which
very few of us are entirely free.
We must be on guard against
this most insidious enemy of our
peace of soul. Instead, let us foster
confidence in God, and thank Him
ahead of time for whatever He
chooses to send us.

Solanus Casey

106

———

Come, let us give a little time to folly...and even in a melancholy day let us find time for an hour of pleasure.

Bonaventure

107

———

We take ourselves too seriously,
and that's the opposite of what
the Gospel message is. We walk
around like the whole world is
on our shoulders. Even at church,
people don't look happy. We
don't look at each other. We're not
connected with each other. And
yet that's what it's all about.

Anne Bryan Smollin

108

When most people go looking for a game changer they usually spend their time and energy looking for that enormous idea that will change everything. But the reality is most game changers are small and simple. It is the simplicity of a game changer that makes implementation and broad adoption possible.

Matthew Kelly

109

___

St. Francis chose peace above all else. He was subject to everyone and every creature and did not fight back. He accepted this—this pacifism, this powerlessness—and he changed the world through it.

Casey Cole

110

———

Both Francis and Clare set a high value on community and our relationships with one another, both within the religious community and with the wider community around us. This means a concern for the common good and a practical interdependence with each other and with the whole earth community. It is a spirituality which is as much about dealing with each other as it is about dealing with God.

Anonymous

111

Franciscans at their best
attempted to live inside the
universal mystery of 'church' and
from there we went out to serve
the world. Most Christians got it
backward by living in the 'world'
and occasionally 'going to church'.

Richard Rohr

112

More than in the countryside, great disparities of wealth and poverty were made conspicuous by the crowded conditions of medieval town life. Meditation on the Gospel and the spectacle of luxury in the midst of destitution led Francis to reject the values of the new urban aristocracy.

Michael Robinson

113

Again I tell you, it is easier for a camel to go through the eye of a needle than for a rich person to enter the kingdom of God.

Matthew 19:24

114

Where there is inner peace
and meditation, there is neither
anxiousness nor dissipation.

Saint Francis of Assisi

115

Do we work on our relationship with God? How do we communicate with God? Are we aware that we're already doing it? And what is that we're actually communicating?

Daniel Horan

116

———

He reacted by literally rebuilding
a dilapidated church. That
was his reaction. But once he
finished rebuilding the church
near his home, he continued to
hear God saying to him, 'Francis,
rebuild my church.' This led him
to the awareness that God was
inviting him to rebuild the church
spiritually. He dedicated the rest
of his life to spiritual renewal.
That was his response.

Matthew Kelly

117

———

He said to them, 'Go into all the world and preach the gospel to all creation.'

Mark 16:15

118

———

Francis of Assisi rejected two central realities of his day: money and warfare. Instead he embraced the joys of simple living, not grasping after the goods money could buy and instead, cherishing the goods that money can't buy.

John D. Bohrer
Joseph M. Stoutzenberger

119

——

Prayer is the best weapon we have; it is the key to God's heart. You must speak to Jesus not only with your lips, but with your heart. If fact, on certain occasions you should only speak to him with your heart.

Padre Pio

120

Jesus did not say, 'Go into all the world and tell the world that it is quite right.'

C. S. Lewis

121

——

By changing the way artists looked at nature and the way human beings looked at each other, Francis helped to spark off one of the greatest revolutions of all time.

Adrian House

122

———

Francis came to discover this fact
that to be a Christian, you couldn't
do this by yourself. He didn't seek a
community at first. He didn't desire
to be the founder of a religious order.
He didn't really want to connect with
other people. He thought it could
just be about him and God. And over
time, he realized that God was going
to break through to him, enter people
into his life, present people to him,
lead people to him that were to form a
community—whether he liked it or not.

William Short

123

———

Everybody needs somebody to share their experiences, their life with. The poor are in need of someone to talk with. Giving people an opportunity to share their life can be quite meaningful for them.

Jason Moore

124

We become what we love and who
we love shapes what we become.
If we love things, we become
a thing. If we love nothing, we
become nothing. Imitation is not a
literal mimicking of Christ, rather
it means becoming the image of
the beloved, an image disclosed
through transformation. This means
we are to become vessels of God's
compassionate love for others.

Saint Clare of Assisi

125

———

 Nobody owns anything but
everyone is rich—for what
greater wealth can there be than
cheerfulness, peace of mind and
freedom from anxiety?

Thomas More

126

All things are possible for him who
believes, more to him who hopes,
even more to him who loves.

Saint Lawrence of Brindisi

127

Blessed is that servant who no more glories in the good said and done in him by the Lord than in that said and done in others.

Saint Francis of Assisi

128

———

Harmony and peace! Francis was a man of harmony and peace. From this City of Peace, I repeat with all the strength and the meekness of love: Let us respect creation, let us not be instruments of destruction! Let us respect each human being. May there be an end to armed conflicts which cover the earth with blood; may the clash of arms be silenced; and everywhere may hatred yield to love, injury to pardon, and discord to unity.

Pope Francis

129

___

Perhaps because he had so often
seen weakness and folly in himself,
Francis was extremely tolerant of it
in others.

John Michael Talbot

130

——

To do with joy the duties
of their calling...

The Third Order of Saint Francis of Assisi

131

I worked with my hands, and I will work still…Let those who know not how, learn, not with the desire of receiving payment for their work, but for a good example and to drive away idleness.

Saint Francis of Assisi

132

Francis determined to be always on the outside what he was on the inside. He knew that some of the brothers felt he overdid this obsession with sincerity and wholeness, but Francis feared duplicity and hypocrisy more than anything in all the world. It was against hypocrisy that Jesus had railed again and again in the Gospels, and Francis was sure Jesus would never speak harshly against anything unless it spoiled the human heart and made the Holy Spirit's entry there impossible.

Murray Bodo

133

___

The real conflict is inner conflict. Beyond armies of occupation and the hecatombs of extermination camps, there are two irreconcilable enemies in the depth of every soul: good and evil, sin and love. And what use are the victories on the battlefield if we ourselves are defeated in our innermost personal selves?

Saint Maximilian Kolbe

134

_____

True reform begins with us. Simply
denouncing the sins of others or of
the Church, real though they may
be, seldom has lasting effect. The
best reform starts with personal
conversion. Personal conversion
spreads to others and then reform is
underway. It works. If we allow God
to set us on fire, then we can spread
that fire.

Charles Pope

135

Francis proclaimed peace where other people proclaimed warnings. Francis proclaimed benevolence and caring and God's love for all when others were proclaiming duty and sacrifice.

Donald Spoto

136

Sanctify yourself and you will sanctify society.

Saint Francis of Assisi

137

———

I went to the woods because I wished to live deliberately, to front only the essential facts of life, and see if I could not learn what it had to teach, and not, when I came to die, discover that I had not lived. I did not wish to live what was not life, living is so dear...I wanted to live deep and suck out all the marrow of life, to live so sturdily and Spartan-like as to put to rout all that was not life...to drive life into a corner, and reduce it to its lowest terms.

Henry David Thoreau

138

The message of St. Francis was uncompromising and simple: greed causes suffering for both the victims and the perpetrators.

Heather McDougall

139

––––

Sooner or later all the people of the world will have to discover a way to live together in peace...If this is to be achieved, man must evolve for all human conflict a method which rejects revenge, aggression and retaliation. The foundation of such a method is love.

Martin Luther King, Jr.

140

_____

Should there anywhere be a brother who comes to seek you, let him not go away, however guilty he may be, without a word of compassion, since he comes for a little.

Saint Francis of Assisi

141

We welcome Jesus by opening our
hearts, homes, and lives to the
friend, the stranger, the lonely, the
lost, the poor, and the confused.

David Pivonka

142

___

I'd rather write about laughing than crying, for laughter makes men human, and courageous.

François Rabelais

143

———

The Christian should be characterized by an effort to see things in the best light; if it is true that the word Evangelos means good news, then Christian means happy man, spreader of happiness.

Pope John Paul I

144

———

Saint Francis and Saint Clare both believed that it is necessary to have a solid experience of community where you share your day, your prayer, your life with one another. It's here that you will grow and stretch. It's this natural human 'give-and-take' where you meet Christ. It's this experience that gives you what it takes to serve others. It is through this balance that you not only change the lives of the people you serve but are also changed yourself.

Jim Moore

145

———

The greatest barrier to loving people, to cherishing people, and to accepting people is our inability to see ourselves in them. Take a closer look.

Matthew Kelly

146

———

Francis and Clare were not so much prophets by what they said as in the radical, system-critiquing way that they lived their lives. They found both their inner and outer freedom by structurally living on the edge of the inside of both church and society. Too often people seek either inner freedom or outer freedom, but seldom...do people find both. They did.

Richard Rohr

147

———

Francis edified his listeners by his example as well as his words...That is, his whole person had become the message he was trying to communicate.

William Short

148

———

Whoever is dependent on his or her money, or worries about it, is truly a poor person. If that person places his or her money at the service of others, then the person becomes very rich, very rich indeed.

Mother Teresa

149

―――

Leave those worldly things that shackle the heart—and very often degrade it—leave all that and come with us in search of love!

Saint Josemaría Escrivá

150

____

We have been called to heal wounds, to unite what has fallen apart, and to bring home those who have lost their way.

Saint Francis of Assisi

151

———

The world cannot give up its dream of universal peace. It is precisely because peace is always coming to be, always incomplete, always fragile, always under attack, always difficult, that we proclaim it. We proclaim it as a duty, an inescapable duty.

Pope Paul VI

152

_____

For me, St. Francis is the man of
poverty, the man of peace, the
man who loves and protects
creation; these days we do not
have a very good relationship with
creation, do we?

Pope Francis

153

___

We have forgotten how to be good
guests, how to walk lightly on the
earth as its other creatures do.

Barbara Ward

154

————

So often I think we're like Francis in the beginning. We think our relationship with God is about us and God alone. But we realize as we grow in our faith that that can't possibly stay the case. That's not the only way to relate to God. That's not what Jesus demonstrates for us. That's not what St. Francis ends up coming around to realize. He realizes that maybe it begins with recognizing this intimate relationship with God…but it extends to others. It models for us the way that we're to relate to others. And that relationship then extends to all of creation too.

Daniel Horan

155

___

The sincere friends of this world
are as ship lights in the stormiest of
nights.

Giotto di Bondone

156

There is a tendency today among some in the radical environmental movement to see man as the enemy of the natural world rather than an integral part of it, to view man as an outsider with respect to the natural world rather than as a partaker and member of it. For St. Francis, though, there was brotherhood.

Charles Pope

157

———

Thousands of tired, nerve-shaken, over-civilized people are beginning to find out that going to the mountains is going home; that wildness is a necessity.

John Muir

158

———

Francis had noticed from the
beginning that when he went
begging, especially, very few people
looked into his eyes. They seemed
always to avoid eye contact, either
from embarrassment or fear or
contempt. There were, of course,
the few bright-eyed, open people
whose eyes were surely the lamps of
their whole selves radiating love and
goodness and trust.

Murray Bodo

159

———

Francis is famous for embracing poverty at any cost, and rightly so. It went hand in hand with the humility that Francis wanted to instill in himself and his brothers. It was also a way of transforming a world that seemed to know only the rule of acquisition at any cost.

Mark Galli

160

_____

Let us love our neighbor as ourselves, and if anyone cannot or will not do so, at least let him do him no evil but seek to do him good.

Saint Francis of Assisi

161

We are formed by the environment
and grace, by politics and prayer,
by church and conscience. All
God's creatures conspire to teach
as well. We stumble. We stutter.
We rise. We are lifted.

Saint Anthony of Padua

162

Spirituality needs to be translated into action. This means a call towards an 'ecological conversion' of the heart which involves gratitude, sobriety and moderation—the ability to be happy with little...It is a call to be less consumeristic, less predatory towards the environment.

Michael Anthony Perry

163

———

The world promises you comfort, but you were not made for comfort. You were made for greatness.

Pope Benedict XVI

164

With his teaching Francis challenged the decadence of church government. He took Jesus's message of nonmaterialism and simplicity seriously, challenging the wealthy and powerful around him.

Rick Steves

165

——

The way to build a church is not
to pay for it, certainly not with
somebody else's money. The way
to build a church is not even to
pay for it with your own money.
The way to build a church is to
build it.

G. K. Chesterton

166

───

When, as a young man, Francis found himself in a fog of doubt as to the nature of God's care for him, he sought the face of God through prayer in solitary places. God opened Francis's eyes of faith.

Jack Wintz

167

Our perfection certainly consists in knowing God and ourselves.

Saint Angela of Foligno

168

Happy...is the servant who does not fill a superior place by his own efforts, but constantly desires to sit at the feet of others.

Saint Francis of Assisi

169

———

That is how the name came into
my heart: Francis of Assisi. For
me, he is the man of poverty, the
man of peace...How I would like a
Church which is poor and for the
poor!

Pope Francis

170

———

The Gospel teaches us that when we care for those in distress we are showing love to Christ himself (cf. Matthew 25:40). Furthermore, when we show loving kindness to the weak and dispossessed we are attuning our hearts to the heart of God in which the poor have a special place. Welcoming outsiders, whether they be people of other cultures or beliefs, immigrants or refugees, is both to love Christ himself, and to love as God loves.

Lewis Thomas Wattson

171

___

If you descend into somebody else's private hell and stand there with them, it ceases to be hell.

Mychal Judge

172

____

It is so easy to make comfort a
priority in our lives...Why doesn't
Jesus want us to get comfortable?
The reason is simple, profound,
and practical: He doesn't want us
to forget that we are just passing
through this world. We are pilgrims.
When we get comfortable we start
to behave as if we are going to live
on this earth forever—and we are
not.

Matthew Kelly

173

What do the Franciscans really have?
The Gospel. That is all.

Daniel Horan

174

The best way to choose what to
keep and what to throw away is to
take each item in one's hand and
ask: 'Does this spark joy?'

Marie Kondō

175

___

The key to living in the midst
of complexity is simplicity.

Matthew Kelly

176

———

There was something about that experience of being intimately related to creation itself that helped Francis grow more fully into the mystery of God. And that's what we are desperately in need of today, because we are so alienated from the earth and from ourselves.

Keith Warner

177

The Holy Rosary, by age-old
tradition, has shown itself
particularly effective as a prayer
which brings the family together.
Individual family members,
in turning their eyes towards
Jesus, also regain the ability to
look one another in the eye, to
communicate, to show solidarity,
to forgive one another and to see
their covenant of love renewed in
the Spirit of God.

Pope John Paul II

178

———

I believe a leaf of grass is no less
than the journey-work of the stars.

Walt Whitman

179

Because children have abounding vitality, because they are in spirit fierce and free, therefore they want things repeated and unchanged. They always say, 'Do it again'...perhaps God is strong enough to exult in monotony. It is possible that God says every morning, 'Do it again' to the sun; and every evening, 'Do it again' to the moon. It may not be automatic necessity that makes all daisies alike; it may be that God makes every daisy separately, but has never got tired of making them. It may be that He has the eternal appetite of infancy; for we have sinned and grown old, and our Father is younger than we.

G. K. Chesterton

180

Christ has something in common
with all creatures. With the stone
he shares existence, with the plants
he shares life, with the animals he
shares sensation, and with the angels
he shares intelligence. Thus all things
are transformed in Christ since in the
fullness of his nature he embraces
some part of every creature.

Bonaventure

181

———

We are his brothers when we do the will of his Father in heaven... and when we bring him forth by holy actions which should enlighten others as an example.

Saint Francis of Assisi

182

_____

Humility exists only in those who are poor enough to see that they possess nothing of their own.

Saint Angela of Foligno

183

The ability to simplify means to eliminate the unnecessary so that the necessary may speak.

Hans Hofmann

184

___

Francis was as much subject to self-doubt as any of us. His motives were purified in prayer; his ego became right-sized there.

Pat McCloskey

185

A sick man can be cured only
by revealing his wounds.

Saint Margaret of Cortona

186

Francis treated all animals
as equals, whether he was
addressing a rabbit, cicada, or a
turtle-dove, or a small donkey.
If they are creatures of God they
were, by definition, his brothers
and sisters.

Agostino Ghilardi

187

———

They are our friends, partners, protectors...ever loyal, all forgiving, to their hearts' last beat. The least we owe them is to live a life that is worthy of their devotion.

Roch

188

If we accept such injustice, such cruelty and such contempt with patience, without being ruffled and without murmuring...
this is perfect joy.

Saint Francis of Assisi

189

———

See everything, overlook a great deal,
correct a little.

Pope John XXIII

190

———

All things created have an order in themselves, and this begets the form that lets the universe resemble God.

Dante

191

——

We need to find God, and he cannot be found in noise and restlessness. God is the friend of silence. See how nature—trees, flowers, grass—grows in silence; see the stars, the moon and the sun, how they move in silence… We need silence to be able to touch souls.

Mother Teresa

192

———

The better part of the man is soon
ploughed into the soil for compost.
By a seeming fate, commonly called
necessity, they are employed, as
it says in an old book, laying up
treasures which moth and rust will
corrupt and thieves break through
and steal. It is a fool's life, as they will
find when they get to the end of it, if
not before.

Henry David Thoreau

193

In Francis's view, property, by arousing envy and, therefore, conflict, was the one thing most destructive to peace in the world.

Joan Acocella

194

There is neither fear nor ignorance where charity and wisdom reign. There is neither anger nor vexation where patience and humility reign.

Saint Francis of Assisi

195

———

Be as a bird perched on a frail
branch that she feels bending
beneath her, still she sings away
all the same, knowing she has
wings.

Victor Hugo

196

———

There's another way...We can recognize our humble place in this universe. We can recognize the silliness of human arrogance and empire. And perhaps as a result, we can learn to appreciate and fully experience the moments that we have as the gifts that they are.

Michael Gungor

197

Great occasions for serving God come seldom, but little ones surround us daily.

Saint Francis de Sales

198

———

What the world needs is a new generation of the people of God who are prepared to abandon the materialism of these modern times. Men and women who know the value of a soul in the context of now and eternity. Men and women who are able to raise their eyes from the things of this world to the greater things of the next world. People who allow Heaven and earth to meet each day in their prayer and in every activity of their lives.

Matthew Kelly

199

———

I am not thinking of reward.
I am working for God and
do so cheerfully.

Saint Marianne Cope

200

———

For Francis and other saints, monastics, and mystics down through the ages, the desire for solitude isn't an effort to flee from the world; it's an attempt to run toward God, to know God better, and to hear God's voice amid the din.

John Michael Talbot

201

We must be faithful to the present moment or we will frustrate the plan of God for our lives.

Solanus Casey

202

_____

The word of God is a light to the mind
and a fire to the will.

Saint Lawrence of Brindisi

203

———

A man who works with his hands is a labourer. A man who works with his hands and his head is a craftsman. A man who works with his hands, his head, and his heart is an artist.

Saint Francis of Assisi

204

———

What was important to him was to live—not without possessions—but without possessing. He was keenly aware of the human person as weak and fragile and thus prone to greed, selfishness and power. To be poor is to live without possessing anything that could prevent true human relatedness as a brother.

Ilia Delio

205

———

Be always patient and full of kindness.
If your brothers do you any wrong,
offer it to God for acceptance. I only
know of one way if you are the servant
of God, which is to bring back the
wandering brother with kindness to
God, and never to cease loving the
brother who sins gravely.

Saint Francis of Assisi

206

——

Do not be afraid; our fate cannot be taken from us; it is a gift.

Dante

207

___

His chief object of concern was to live free from all things that are in the world, so that his inner serenity would not be disturbed even for a moment by contact with any of its dust.

Thomas of Celano

208

_____

Human attitudes and behavior
toward creation directly reflect
human attitudes of behavior
toward other people.

Sister Francisca

209

___

We are made loveless
by our possessions.

Saint Elizabeth of Hungary

210

The cross is the school of love.

Saint Maximilian Kolbe

211

___

The persons who annoy you,
brothers or others, even if they
should go so far as to strike you, all
this you should regard as a favor.
Desire only that and nothing else.

Saint Francis of Assisi

212

———

Be souls of prayer. Never tire
of praying, it is what is essential.
Prayer shakes the heart of God;
it obtains necessary graces!

Padre Pio

213

What happens to the drop of wine
That you pour into the sea?
Does it remain itself, unchanged?
It is as if it never existed.
So it is with the soul:
Love drinks it in,
It is united with Truth,
Its old nature fades away,
It is no longer master of itself.

Jacopone da Todi

214

———

There is nothing more inglorious
than the glory that is gained by war.

Saint Thomas More

215

———

Truly, matters in the world are in a bad state; but if you and I begin in earnest to reform ourselves, a really good beginning will have been made.

Saint Peter of Alcantara

216

For poverty is that heavenly virtue
by which all earthy and transitory
things are trodden under foot,
and by which every obstacle is
removed from the soul so that it
may freely enter into union with
the eternal Lord God. It is also
the virtue which makes the soul,
while still here on earth, converse
with the angels in Heaven.

Saint Francis of Assisi

217

Jesus told him, 'If you want to be perfect, go, sell your possessions and give to the poor, and you will have treasure in heaven.'

Matthew 19:21

218

——

Since happiness is nothing else than
the enjoyment of the Supreme Good,
and the Supreme Good is above us,
no one can enjoy happiness unless
he rises above himself.

Bonaventure

219

As St. Francis did not love humanity
but men, so he did not love
Christianity but Christ.

G. K. Chesterton

220

To ask the proper question
is half of knowing.

Roger Bacon

221

How are you being challenged
to conversion?

Greg Friedman

222

———

Many people regarded him as
mad…Francis accepted all this
serenely, and the qualities that at
the beginning had marked him as
an eccentric eventually made him
seem holy.

Joan Acocella

223

———

The only thing ever achieved in life
without effort is failure.

Saint Francis of Assisi

224

———

Freedom is not the ability to do whatever you want. Freedom is the strength of character to do what is good, true, noble, and right. Freedom is the ability to choose and celebrate the-best-version-of-yourself in every moment.

Matthew Kelly

225

———

God desires, not death but faith.
God thirsts, not for blood but for
self-surrender. God is appeased,
not by slaughter but by the
offering of your free will.

Saint Joseph of Cupertino

226

In company, guard your tongue.
In your family, guard your temper.
When alone, guard your thoughts.

Matt Talbot

227

___

The devil is afraid of us when we pray and make sacrifices. He is also afraid when we are humble and good. He is especially afraid when we love Jesus very much.

Saint Anthony of Padua

228

Blessed is the religious who finds his
pleasure and joy in holy discourse
and the works of the Lord, and who,
by these means, leads men to the
love of God with joy and gladness.

Saint Francis of Assisi

229

———

Francis and Clare were like
enlightened modern millennials,
young 'Christocentric' idealistic
leaders desiring a better world, who
through their example preaching and
living the Gospel inspired others to
follow the footsteps of Christ.

Noel Irwin Hentschel

230

———

Poverty alone guards the armor
of true humility and charity.

Saint Francis of Assisi

231

The creator of the heavens obeys a carpenter; the God of eternal glory listens to a poor virgin. Has anyone ever witnessed anything comparable to this? Let the philosopher no longer disdain from listening to the common laborer; the wise, to the simple; the educated,to the illiterate; a child of a prince, to a peasant.

Saint Anthony of Padua

232

———

The view is quite often expressed by preachers today that the problem with our western society is that we are too materialistic, that we overvalue the material at the expense of the spiritual. Francis, I think, would rather say that we are not nearly materialist enough. We take material things too lightly, we show no reverence towards creation; we take it for granted.

Brother Samuel

233

We should work for simple, good, undecorated things, but things which are in harmony with the human being and organically suited to the little man in the street.

Alvar Aalto

234

___

But Francis would not let them
accept any money. He told them
to treat coins as if they were
pebbles in the road. When the
bishop showed horror at the friars'
hard life, Francis said, 'If we had
any possessions we should need
weapons and laws to defend them.'
Possessing something was the
death of love for Francis.

Anonymous

235

———

It turns out more stuff doesn't make us happier, especially when we factor in the extra time we have to work to pay for it and maintain it, even the time we spend just looking for it in our stuff-filled drawers and cupboards and homes.

Annie Leonard

236

___

These concepts of universal brotherhood and respect of human dignity are also reflected in Francis' pursuit of peace, nonviolence, and dialogue. During the Fifth Crusade, in 1219, Francis travelled to Damietta, Egypt, where he met with Malik al-Kamil, the Sultan of Egypt...He attempted to broker peace between warring factions by bringing a message of peace. Although his effort ultimately failed, Francis showed the extent of his repudiation of hostility and violence, and his understanding of universal kinship— the belief in our inherent dignity and worth as brothers and sisters.

Anonymous

237

─────

Love your enemies, do good to those who hate you, bless those who curse you, and pray for those who mistreat you.

Luke 6:27-28

238

————

As 'pride is the beginning of all sin,' (Eccl. x, 15) so humility is the foundation of all virtue. Learn to be really humble and not, as the hypocrite, humble merely in appearance.

Bonaventure

239

———

How could I bear a crown of gold
when the Lord bears a crown of
thorns? And bears it for me!

Saint Elizabeth of Hungary

240

———

That's the work of a prophet—
to point out how we've gotten it
wrong and how we can transform
ourselves and our world.

John D. Bohrer
Joseph M. Stoutzenberger

241

————

He advised his followers that in going about the world 'they should not be quarrelsome or take part in disputes with words...or criticize others; but they should be gentle, peaceful and unassuming, courteous and humble, speaking respectfully to everyone... Whatever house they enter, they should first say, "Peace to this house"' (Cf. Luke 10:5). Surely, Francis was an instrument of peace.

Jack Wintz

242

By the anxieties and worries
of this life Satan tries to dull
man's heart and make a
dwelling for himself there.

Saint Francis of Assisi

243

___

Instead, Francis chose a radical life of caring for the poor through his acts of love and humility where he lived among lepers, homeless and others that were neglected by society. Francis was a tough and demanding revolutionary voyager of the human spirit.

Victor Narro

244

_____

Pride thinks it's own happiness
shines the brighter by comparing it
with the misfortunes of others.

Saint Thomas More

245

___

As long as you are looking down
you cannot see something
that is above you.

C. S. Lewis

246

———

When we're grateful, we open up our hearts, and our attitudes are much more positive. We have to make conscious choices to surround ourselves with positive attitudes—to be people of gratitude. Those are choices. And if you make healthier choices, what we're doing is really and truly living out the joyful Gospel message.

Anne Bryan Smollin

247

———

Without humility of heart, all the other virtues by which one runs toward God seem—and are—absolutely worthless.

Saint Angela of Foligno

248

———

Be praised, my Lord, through those
who forgive for love of you; through
those who endure sickness and trial.
Happy are those who endure in
peace, for they will be crowned.

Saint Francis of Assisi

249

Now there is great gain in
godliness with contentment, for
we brought nothing into the world,
and we cannot take anything out
of the world.

1 Timothy 6:6-8

250

———

When people look for identity
and meaning in the marketplace,
they'll never really find themselves.

Daniel Horan

251

Do not get any gold or silver or copper to take with you in your belts—no bag for the journey or extra shirt or sandals or a staff, for the worker is worth his keep.

Matthew 10:9

252

———

Chaotic and intuitive, creative and affectionate, radical and obedient, the Franciscan tradition may offer to those searching for a 'path' of spirituality an appealing itinerary.

William Short

253

Keep your face always toward
the sunshine—and shadows
will fall behind you.

Walt Whitman

254

_____

The key to it all for Francis was
his sense of 'giftedness'; he was
overwhelmed by the generosity of
God in and through creation and he
lived in a constant state
of grateful dependence.

Brother Samuel

255

Charity is the soul of faith, makes it alive.

Saint Anthony of Padua

256

———

For when I was in sin, it was very
bitter for me to see lepers; but the
Lord Himself led me into the midst
of them, and I practiced mercy
towards them. And when I was in their
presence, what had before seemed
bitter to me was changed into
sweetness of soul and body.

Saint Francis of Assisi

257

Never be too hard on the man who can't give up drink. It's as hard to give up drink as it is to raise the dead to life again. But both are possible and even easy for Our Lord. We have only to depend on Him.

Matt Talbot

258

———

Many are faithful at prayer and at the Divine Office...but let them suffer an injury, let them be deprived of something, and they will immediately be offended and troubled. This is not to be poor in spirit.

Saint Francis of Assisi

259

——

Chastity without charity
is a lamp without oil.

Bonaventure

260

Francis' desire to share his spirituality and message of peace with the Sultan, without insulting Islam or refuting Mohammed, was unique and disarming. During that brief moment in history where Francis and Sultan al-Kamil were with one another, their dialogue turned into an embrace of each other as human beings driven by their religious belief for a higher good.

Victor Narro

261

———

While you are proclaiming peace
with your lips, be careful to have it
even more fully in your heart.

Saint Francis of Assisi

262

St. Francis offers a vision of a different world, where we share more equally the abundant wealth of goods and life itself as we focus on the right relations to the earth.

Heather McDougall

263

Francis abandoned riches and comfort
in order to become a poor man
among the poor. He understood that
true joy and riches do not come from
the idols of this world—material things
and the possession of them—but are
to be found only in following Christ
and serving others.

Pope Francis

264

_____

One cannot estimate how much
interior patience and humility the
servant of God possesses while he is
happy. But when the time comes that
those who ought to be amiable to
him are the contrary, then he shows
as much patience and humility as he
truly possesses, and nothing more.

Saint Francis of Assisi

265

Love that cannot suffer
is not worthy of the name.

Saint Clare of Assisi

266

What, my dear brothers, is more
delightful than the voice of
the Lord calling to us?

Saint Benedict the Moor

267

Why is Francis still a symbol of peace for people of many faiths today? While numerous answers are possible, five can be highlighted: ecumenism, peace, justice, forgiveness and prayer. Together, all five can help us understand Francis's singular desire to follow in the footsteps of our Lord Jesus.

Jay Hammond

268

During all its long life, our live oak never took more than it needed. It never gorged itself on water or gobbled more nutrients than it required. What would the world's environment be like today if the human race had been as temperate as oaks?

Kenneth Davis

269

It makes sense that God created
us dependent on them, so that we
would not abuse and destroy them.
Perhaps the idea in the mind of God
was, if we were dependent on the
other elements of nature, we would
respect and live in harmony with
them.

Matthew Kelly

270

Spiritual joy arises from purity of the heart and perseverance in prayer.

Saint Francis of Assisi

271

—

They have not changed much since the time of Saint Francis. Even now these places contain many caves and grottoes, covered with deep woods, and broken by ravines and gorges. The grottoes were the actual dwellings of Francis and his first companions. Here, in the silence of these wild retreats, they prolonged their dialogue with God.

Agostino Ghilardi

272

Francis saw everything as dramatic, distinct from its setting, not all of a piece like a picture but in action like a play. A bird went by him like an arrow; something with a story and a purpose.

G. K. Chesterton

273

___

What great lessons can nature teach us about ourselves? Nature whispers messages to us each and every day: 'Great things are achieved little by little. Discover the rhythm of life and align your life with this rhythm. The more you do, the more you will enjoy peace and prosperity.'

Matthew Kelly

274

The essence of Franciscan spirituality, then, is a focus on seeing God in everyone, especially the marginalized, and working toward protecting the integrity of all creation...with particular emphasis on the poor, vulnerable, and those least responsible for environmental degradation.

Kelly Moltzen

275

———

Be as wise as Brother Daisy and
Brother Dandelion; for never
do they lie awake thinking of
tomorrow, yet they have gold
crowns like kings and emperors.

G. K. Chesterton

276

Happy persons seldom think of happiness. They are too busy losing their lives in the meaningful sacrifices of service.

David Augsburger

277

Let us be charitable and humble,
let us give alms and wash our soul
from the stains of sin. Man loses
all he leaves in this world, but he
takes away with him the fruits of his
charity and the alms
he has scattered.

Saint Francis of Assisi

278

In addition to being a prophet, Francis had an artist's spirit. He was a poet and a songwriter, and his life was something like that of a performance artist. If he advocated poverty and simplicity, he lived it. If he called for peace, he intervened where there was conflict. If he said to strip yourself of your possessions, he modeled it himself. If he saw beauty in nature, he actually communed with nature as few people ever have.

John D. Bohrer
Joseph M. Stoutzenberger

279

———

To know much and taste nothing—
of what use is that?

Bonaventure

280

———

Those who are marginalized
have a special place in the
hearts of Franciscans...Francis
and Clare experienced the
poor Christ in the least, the
suffering, and even in their own
frailty.

Anonymous

281

———

But with every passing day, God
is gently inviting us to live more
generously, calling us to switch the
focus off ourselves and onto others.
'It is better to give than receive.' (Acts
20:35) The more we are mindful of
how much we have received, the
more we are inclined to look for
opportunities to give.

Matthew Kelly

282

———

Francis was acutely conscious of the pervasive divine presence, making the whole world a theatre for the praise of the Creator. No longer was the parish church deemed to be the only place where the things of God were aired…Francis found the divine footprints everywhere and wished to bring his neighbors to a greater recognition of their Creator.

Michael J. P. Robson

283

———

It was easy to love God in all that
was beautiful. The lessons of deeper
knowledge, though, instructed me
to embrace God in all things.

Saint Francis of Assisi

284

The cultural environment of our contemporary society, especially here in the U.S., provides the conditions to lure away or distract us from confronting and embracing who we really are, ultimately leaving us to settle for the allurements for what is so often our consumer-driven society.

Daniel Horan

285

___

For where your treasure is,
there your heart will be also

Matthew 6:21

286

What I believe Francis would
want more than anything is
for you to turn more deeply to
Jesus and to realize that every
one of us are called to be saints.
The word 'saint' simply means
faithful ones.

Keith Fournier

287

———

The ordinary arts we practice
every day at home are of more
importance to the soul than their
simplicity might suggest.

Saint Thomas More

288

———

As he saw it now, the more a person was despised, the more he or she resembled Jesus in his last agonies, when he was abandoned by almost all the people he had come to save. To obey Jesus, therefore, you had to join those who were abandoned.

Joan Acocella

289

———

Jesus wants you to become the most generous person in your sphere of influence. He wants to astonish people with your generosity. He wants you to be generous with your time, talent, and treasure. But he invites you to a generosity that goes far beyond these. He wants you to be generous with your praise and encouragement. He wants you to be generous with your compassion and patience. He wants generosity to reach into every area of your life so that through you he can love and intrigue the people in your life.

Matthew Kelly

290

———

It is not enough to think of different species merely as potential 'resources' to be exploited, while overlooking the fact that they have value in themselves.

Pope Francis

291

Every human action leaves a lasting
imprint on the body of the earth.

Sister Francisca

292

These experiences of Incarnation—of
cross and crib and of Eucharist—both
inspire and impel Francis to live
his life in imitation of this Christ:
the poor and suffering one who,
in his human condition, could be
recognized as neighbor and brother.

Zachary Hayes

293

He did not consider himself at the top of hierarchy of being nor did he declare himself superior to non-human creation. Rather, Francis saw himself as part of creation. His spirituality overturned the spirituality of hierarchical ascent and replaced it with a spirituality of descending solidarity between humanity and creation.

Ilia Delio

294

_____

Give to the one who begs from you,
and do not turn away from the one
who wants to borrow from you.

Saint Francis of Assisi

295

We have the same natural abilities
that were in Jesus Christ: his ability to
love God and others with generosity
is our ability to love God and
others with generosity. His ability to
welcome the stranger reflects our
own ability, or rather our vocation to
look beyond our own communities
to see others in the light of our bond
with them. This bond, then, must be
expressed through concrete actions:
hospitable deeds, actions of care, of
generosity and of solidarity, in order
to develop the right relations, which
is the true meaning of justice.

Michael A. Perry

296

Earthly riches are like the
reed. Its roots are sunk in
the swamp, and its exterior
is fair to behold; but inside it
is hollow. If a man leans on
such a reed, it will snap off
and pierce his soul.

Saint Anthony of Padua

297

___

If honor were profitable,
everybody would be honorable.

Saint Thomas More

298

Saint Francis of Assisi bears witness to the need to respect all that God has created and as he created it, without manipulating and destroying creation; rather to help it grow, to become more beautiful and more like what God created it to be.

Pope Francis

299

———

There is no sin in consuming; humans can't photosynthesize, after all. Nor in using earth's bounty...but there are limits, and they are being transgressed...It makes me want to call out, too: 'Can you hear me, Saint Francis?' Or more to the point: 'Can I hear you?'

Kennedy Warne

300

———

It is no use walking anywhere to preach
unless our walking is our preaching.

Saint Francis of Assisi

301

What does it matter where we go?
Wherever we go, won't we be
serving God there? And wherever
we go, won't we have Our Lord
in the Blessed Sacrament with
us? Isn't that enough to make us
happy?

Solanus Casey

302

——

He comes to remind the world
that the welfare of man, the peace
of his heart, the joy of his life, are
neither in money, nor in learning,
nor in strength, but in an upright
and sincere will.

Paul Sabatier

303

We must never see suffering as a proof of God's absence. Rather, we must see with St. Francis of Assisi that God works through our suffering, teaching us to love, to trust, and to bear our burden with humility and patience.

Joseph Mary Elder

304

———

Francis had the capacity to go deep into someone's heart and share the joy and sadness of that person. As activists, we too have the potential to connect through our hearts and let that connection be the driving force that enables us to struggle together, to strategize together, and to win together. After all, this is true solidarity in action— our interconnectedness with one other, the spiritual force of love and compassion for one another, much in the same way of the unconditional love that Francis had for all of creation.

Victor Narro

305

_____

Generosity and forgiveness are
two of the most radical invitations
the Gospel makes. They are also
among the most difficult to live.

Matthew Kelly

306

———

A monk asks: Is there anything more miraculous than the wonders of nature?

The master answers: Yes, your awareness of the wonders of nature.

Angelus Silesius

307

His joy and wonder increased as he carefully admonished them to listen to the Word of God: 'My brother birds, you should greatly praise your Creator and love Him always. He clothed you with feathers and gave you wings for flying. Among all His creatures He made you free and gave you the purity of the air. You neither sow nor reap, He nevertheless governs you without your least care.'

Thomas of Celano

308

———

My dear son, be patient, because the weaknesses of the body are given to us in this world by God for the salvation of the soul. So they are of great merit when they are borne patiently.

Saint Francis of Assisi

309

_____

True humility is not thinking less
of yourself; it is thinking of yourself
less.

C. S. Lewis

310

———

In times of desolation, God conceals Himself from us so that we can discover for ourselves what we are without Him.

Saint Margaret of Cortona

311

———

I believe it's possible for everyone to discover this silence within themselves. It is there all the time, even when we are surrounded by constant noise. Deep down in the ocean, below the waves and ripples, you can find your internal silence. Standing in the shower, letting the water wash over your head, sitting in front of a crackling fire, swimming across a forest lake or taking a walk over a field: all these can be experiences of perfect stillness too.

Erling Kagge

312

———

The trees and the earth, water
and air, every atom and molecule
in existence is infused with the
goodness of God's creative power
and holds the potential of God's
presence.

Casey Cole

313

___

Blessed be God in all his designs.

Solanus Casey

314

———

Most of the luxuries and many of
the so-called comforts of life are
not only not indispensable, but
positive hindrances to the elevation
of mankind.

Henry David Thoreau

315

———

Nothing you have not given away
will ever really be yours.

C. S. Lewis

316

———

Francis strove to be Christlike.
He taught by example, he lived
without worldly goods and
loved all of creation.

Rick Steves

317

———

I beg you then, with all possible respect, not to forget the Lord nor to swerve from His commandments in the midst of the cares and anxieties of this world.

Saint Francis of Assisi

318

———

In the silence of prayer, we can hear the symphony of creation calling us to abandon our self-centeredness in order to feel embraced by the tender love of the Father and to share with joy the gifts we have received.

Pope Francis

319

———

For everything created by God is good,
and nothing is to be rejected if it is
received with thanksgiving.

1 Timothy 4:4

320

———

The best remedy for those who are afraid, lonely or unhappy is to go outside, somewhere where they can be quite alone with the heavens, nature and God. Because only then does one feel that all is as it should be and that God wishes to see people happy, amidst the simple beauty of nature. As longs as this exists, and it certainly always will, I know that then there will always be comfort for every sorrow, whatever the circumstances may be. And I firmly believe that nature brings solace in all troubles.

Anne Frank

321

God called the dry land Earth, and the waters that were gathered together he called Seas. And God saw that it was good.

Genesis 1:10

322

———

This is My commandment,
that you love one
another, as I have loved
you.

John 15:12

323

———

Happy is the religious who loves
his brother who is sick and unable
to be useful to him as much as he
loves him who is well and capable
of doing service. Happy the
brother who loves and respects
his own absent brother as much as
if he were present.

Saint Francis of Assisi

324

In all your deeds and words you should look upon this Jesus as your model. Do so whether you are walking or keeping silence, or speaking, whether you are alone or with others. He is perfect, and thus you will be not only irreprehensible, but praiseworthy.

Bonaventure

325

———

Do not pray for easy lives; pray to
be stronger people. Do not pray for
tasks equal to your powers; pray for
powers equal to your tasks.

Solanus Casey

326

———

The poor man of Assisi gives
us striking witness that when
we are at peace with God
we are better able to devote
ourselves to building up that
peace with all creation which is
inseparable from peace among
all peoples.

Pope John Paul II

327

___

Feeding the birds is also
a form of prayer.

Pope Pius XII

328

___

Nothing is so strong as gentleness;
nothing so gentle as real strength.

Saint Francis de Sales

329

The things we pray for, good Lord,
give us the grace to labor for.

Saint Thomas More

330

_____

He has sent you into the whole world to give witness to His word by your own word and by your deeds, and to make known to all that there is none other almighty but He.

Saint Francis of Assisi

331

——

Francis used to view the largest crowd as if it were a single person, and he would preach fervently to a single person as if to a large crowd.

Thomas of Celano

332

———

No man putting his hand to the plough and looking back is fit for the kingdom of God.

Luke 9:62

333

———

The journey is essential to the dream.

Saint Francis of Assisi

334

———

Neutralize inflamed conversations
by presuming that those with
whom we differ are acting in good
faith. Collaborate with others
and recognize that all human
engagement is an opportunity to
promote peace.

Mary Jo Chaves

335

——

Those are truly peacemakers
who, in the midst of all their
sufferings, in the midst of the
world, preserve exterior and
interior peace for the love of our
Lord Jesus Christ.

Saint Francis of Assisi

336

———

Wake up and look around. Get grateful. Focus on the basics. Start living again. You see life is for living, and the best living is done amid the ordinary things of each day.

Matthew Kelly

337

Jesus, help me to simplify my life by learning what you want me to be and becoming that person.

Saint Thérèse of Lisieux

338

___

Like Francis, we are called to
be attentive to each of our
relationships, to each person
we encounter, to the tiniest
particulars of our lives. For Francis,
attention meant sensitivity and
connectedness, which showed him
the joys and sorrows of the world.

Marcella Nachreiner

339

___

Because he was very humble, he showed meekness to all people, and duly adapted himself to the behavior of all. Holy among holy, among sinners he was like one of them.

Thomas of Celano

340

_____

When you have stabilized your heart
in right faith, and steadfast hope,
and perfect love, then you will heave
up your heart in high contemplation
of your Creator.

Saint Francis of Assisi

341

___

Lord, take me where You want
me to go, let me meet who You
want me to meet, tell me what
You want me to say, and keep me
out of your way.

Mychal Judge

342

———

True progress quietly and
persistently moves along without
notice.

Saint Francis of Assisi

343

_____

The best perfection of a religious man is to do common things in a perfect manner. A constant fidelity in small things is a great and heroic virtue.

Bonaventure

344

———

The greatest danger for most
of us is not that our aim is
too high and we miss it, but
that it is too low and we
reach it.

Michelangelo

345

———

In the grand spectacles of nature there is something divine; from it our minds and hearts gain a virtue at once pacifying and encouraging, we experience the salutary sensation of littleness, and seeing the beauties and the sadnesses of the past we learn better how to judge the present hour.

Paul Sabatier

346

———

Have patience with all things—
but first with yourself. Never
confuse your mistakes with
your value as a human being.

Saint Francis de Sales

347

God could not have chosen anyone less qualified, or more of a sinner, than myself. And so, for this wonderful work He intends to perform through us, He selected me—for God always choses the weak and the absurd, and those who count for nothing.

Saint Francis of Assisi

348

———

Let us make the very best use of the precious moments and do all in our power for His dear sake and for His greater honor and glory.

Saint Marianne Cope

349

I know many that could not
when they should because they
did not when they could.

François Rabelais

350

___

Everyone loves Francis, not just
Christians. Christians and non-
Christians, men and women of
great faith, men and women of
no faith love Francis of Assisi.
And I think the reason is because
there's nothing more attractive
than holiness.

Matthew Kelly

351

When I don't know what's next, I
get down on my knees and pray,
Lord, take me, mold me, fashion
me, show me what You want. Then
I watch and listen, and it will come.

Mychal Judge

352

_____

Every creature is a divine word
because it proclaims God.

Bonaventure

353

Francis was foremost a follower
of Jesus, but in him there was no
tension between loving God and
loving all creatures of God.

Anonymous

354

———

This crisis is the result of us
not living the Christian faith
dynamically. This has been
furthered by our desperate need
to be loved and accepted, which
has led us to choose to live in
ways that cause us to blend
in with people of no faith. The
first Christians differentiated
themselves from society. Modern
Christians blend in.

Matthew Kelly

355

___

Let us all remember this: one cannot proclaim the Gospel of Jesus without the tangible witness of one's life. Those who listen to us and observe us must be able to see in our actions what they hear from our lips, and so give glory to God! I am thinking now of some advice that Saint Francis of Assisi gave his brothers: preach the Gospel and, if necessary, use words. Preaching with your life, with your witness.

Pope Francis

356

The future has several names. For the weak, it is impossible; for the fainthearted, it is unknown; but for the valiant, it is ideal.

Victor Hugo

357

———

Strength and guidance. That's all
I'm wishing for, my friends.

Saint Francis of Assisi

358

———

To know each other is the best way to understand each other. To understand each other is the only way to love each other.

Michelangelo

359

They call us romantics...sentimental idealists, perhaps because we have some faith in the good which exists even in our opponents.

Fridtjof Nansen

360

———

Remember when you leave this earth, you can take with you nothing that you have received, only what you have given: a heart enriched in host service, love, sacrifice and courage.

Saint Francis of Assisi

361

Go forth in peace, for you have
followed the good road. Go forth
without fear, for he who created
you has made you holy, has always
protected you.

Saint Clare of Assisi

362

Always forward, never back.

Saint Junipero Serra

363

___

Grant that I may not so much seek
to be consoled as to console, to be
understood as to understand, to be
loved as to love. For it is in giving that
we receive, it is in pardoning that we
are pardoned, and it is in dying that
we are born to eternal life.

Saint Francis of Assisi

364

Consult not your fears but your hopes and your dreams. Think not about your frustrations, but about your unfulfilled potential. Concern yourself not with what you tried and failed in, but with what it is still possible for you to do.

Pope John XXIII

365

A single sunbeam is enough
to drive away many shadows.

Saint Francis of Assisi